LET ME ADJUST MY CROWN AND GO GET MY PURPOSE

LET ME Adjust my Crown

AND GO GET MY PURPOSE

Sheila Prioleau

Palmetto
PUBLISHING GROUP

Palmetto Publishing Group
Charleston, SC

Let Me Adjust My Crown and Go Get My Purpose

Copyright © 2018 by Sheila Prioleau

First Edition

Printed in the United States

ISBN-13: 978-1-64111-141-6
ISBN-10: 1-64111-141-0

Dedication

To my lovely daughter, Shayla Prioleau, I love you with my all my heart. I dedicate this book to you. I want you to stay true to yourself because you are amazing. Love, encourage, and give yourself the affirmation every day, regardless of what the day or your surrounding may bring.

Always put God first in your life and in every life decision you make. Find your passion—your heart's desire—for it will lead you to your purpose. Pursue your goal with every fiber of your being. Without it, life holds no real meaning. Love others irrespective of their flaws or the mistakes they may make. More importantly, forgive, forgive, forgive. Forgiveness does not come easily, but if you cling on to being unforgiving, you will be held captive by the anger it brings. Forgiving others and yourself will set your soul free. Release it, so that you can live a purposeful life without regrets.

Table of Contents

Foreword

In August 1982, I met two of the most important individuals in my life: my husband and Sheila. Sheila soon became my best friend/sister. We have now known each other for more than half of our lives. Who would you lend your wedding dress to other than your daughter? Your best friend, that's who!

When I was asked to write this foreword, I immediately accepted it as an absolute honor.

So how do you define a friend? According to the dictionary, the word "friend" describes a person one knows, with whom one shares a bond of mutual affection and interests.

Allow me to add that a friend is also someone who will not only unhesitatingly tell you that your crown is tilted, but will also help you straighten it! A friend is someone who accepts you for all you are and understands that you are the sum of your perfect imperfections. A true friend is a person who knows that you are a queen and will never allow you to descend from your throne to deal with unroyal behavior. My friend—no, my sister. Sheila is beautiful, empowered, and extraordinary.

With heartiest congratulations and love,
Leste (Celeste M. Jordan)

Preface

Let Me Adjust My Crown and Go Get My Purpose is a self-help journal to help young girls self-evaluate, self-reflect, and self-examine their potential, passion, values, characteristics, and principles, so they find out their purpose and their mission in life.

Let your determination, your heart's desire, grant you a reason to wake up in the morning and handle each day like a queen. Let each day get you closer to your path of purpose. I hope that this journal will shine a little light on that journey. Let it be a guide that aids you in your life's decisions. Let it inspire good behavior, shape your aspirations, and offer you a sense of direction towards purposeful living.

During your study and after, for any questions or comments, please email me at beequeen414@gmail.com

"You may encounter many defeats, but you must not be defeated. In fact, it may be necessary to encounter the defeats, so you can know who you are, what you can rise from, how you can still come out of."

–Maya Angelou

Reflection I

Dear Mirror on the Wall am I a **QUEEN** to be called?

Every day, I stare into the mirror, asking myself the same questions over and over again: Who am I? Is this life worth living? Am I a positive influence on someone else? Will I be able to brave tough situations? Am I good enough? Am I living without a purpose? What is my goal?

I speak to the mirror as though it comprehends my questions. Why are you silent? Why do you merely stare at me? How long am I to wait before you answer my questions?

This silence troubled me. Then, I hear a small, soft voice say, "Only you can answer these questions. It's your life, and you must find your purpose. Only you can discover your true purpose in life—the reason you are here in the first place. Only you can answer why you exist. Why do you wait for others to validate your existence? Are you defined by what they think of you?"

No matter how much you try, you cannot possibly hide from your inner self. Others only perceive that which stands before them; they can see only your exterior. It's up to you to find your inner peace and happiness. You alone can discover the purpose that lies within you. Get up, go out, adjust your crown, and run to your goal.

WEEK 1

"And who knows but that you have come to your royal position for such a time as this?"

– Esther 4:14

Introduction - The Book of Esther

Esther 4:14

Esther, a young Jewish orphan, is the heroine of this story. Her life is full of action, drama, and romance. Esther's story is the kind of stuff movies and best-seller novels were made from. It is a true story—the saga of how this young girl went from rags to riches. Despite who she was, despite her circumstances and situations. God saw it fit to use Esther for saving His people. She had not gone to the palace with thoughts of becoming a queen or a heroine for God's people. She was merely at the right place at the right time. She was divinely positioned by God to fulfill His purpose for her life.

Esther was confronted with many obstacles—death threats, her fear, and the hatred toward the Jews—during her time in the palace. However, even in the face of adversities, Esther waited with purpose and God supplied her every need. Esther took a risk and even though she felt outnumbered and powerless, she allowed God to guide her through the circumstances that were present before her. The Book of Esther shows God's divine guidance and His love and care for His people. It also highlights Esther's purpose in life. Esther might not have known her purpose when she first went to the palace but, it was her faith and trust in God that kept her.

Let Esther life speak to your heart. It was not about where Esther was from, who her family was or was not. It was about what God saw in her and not any-one else. You were designed for a purpose, for God's use.

"Don't let anyone rob you of your imagination, your creativity, or your curiosity. It's your place in the world; it's your life. Go on and do all you can with it, and make it the life you want to live."
– Mae Jemison

Esther's Life

Day 1

- ♥ **God's Plan**
  - ❧ Jeremiah 29:11
  - ❧ Psalm 27:14

Day 2

- ♥ **God's Purpose**
  - ❧ Ecclesiastes 12:13-14
  - ❧ Exodus 9:16

Day 3

- ♥ **Walk in unity**
  - ❧ Psalm 133:1
  - ❧ Philippians 2:2

Day 4

- ♥ **Determination—don't quit**
  - ❧ I Corinthians 9:24-27
  - ❧ Philippians 4:13

Day 5

- ♥ **Fasting and Praying**
  - ❧ Matthew 17:20-21
  - ❧ Ezra 8:23

Be perfectly
imperfect.

God's Plan

Read each scripture and explain in your own words what each one means to you.

Jeremiah 29:11 _____

_____

_____

_____

_____

_____

_____

_____

_____

_____

Psalm 27:14 _____

_____

_____

_____

_____

_____

_____

_____

_____

_____

_____

From your reading of the Book of Esther, provide a summary and the moral of the story.

Summary: _____

_____

_____

_____

_____

_____

_____

_____

_____

_____

_____

_____

Moral: _____

_____

_____

_____

_____

_____

_____

_____

_____

_____

_____

_____

What was God's plan for Esther? _____

_____

_____

_____

_____

_____

_____

_____

_____

_____

_____

_____

_____

Should you always have a plan? Why or why not? _____

_____

_____

_____

_____

_____

_____

_____

_____

_____

_____

_____

_____

_____

What is the importance of God's timing in our lives? _____

_____

_____

_____

_____

_____

_____

_____

_____

_____

_____

_____

_____

_____

_____

_____

God's Purpose

Read each scripture and explain in your own words what each one means to you.

Ecclesiastes 12:13-14 _____

_____

_____

_____

_____

_____

_____

_____

_____

_____

Exodus 9:16 _____

_____

_____

_____

_____

_____

_____

_____

_____

_____

_____

Who was Esther? How did Esther become a queen? _____

_____

_____

_____

_____

_____

_____

_____

_____

_____

_____

_____

_____

What was Esther's purpose? _____

_____

_____

_____

_____

_____

_____

_____

_____

_____

_____

_____

_____

_____

What does it mean to have purpose in your life? _____

_____
_____
_____
_____
_____
_____
_____
_____
_____
_____
_____
_____
_____

Do you think God has a purpose for your life? Why or why not? _____

_____
_____
_____
_____
_____
_____
_____
_____
_____
_____
_____
_____
_____

Walk in Unity

Read each scripture and explain in your own words what each one means to you.

Psalm 133:1 _____

_____

_____

_____

_____

_____

_____

_____

_____

_____

Philippians 2:2 _____

_____

_____

_____

_____

_____

_____

_____

_____

_____

_____

Who was Queen Vashti and what happened to her? _____

_____

_____

_____

_____

_____

_____

_____

_____

_____

_____

_____

Why did Esther call the people to fast and pray? _____

_____

_____

_____

_____

_____

_____

_____

_____

_____

_____

_____

_____

What does it mean to walk with God? _____

_____

_____

_____

_____

_____

_____

_____

_____

_____

_____

_____

_____

When you don't agree with others, does it create an issue? Why or why not?

_____

_____

_____

_____

_____

_____

_____

_____

_____

_____

_____

_____

_____

Determination/Don't Quit

Read each scripture and explain in your own words what each one means to you.

I Corinthians 9:24-27 _____

_____

_____

_____

_____

_____

_____

_____

_____

_____

_____

Philippians 4:13 _____

_____

_____

_____

_____

_____

_____

_____

_____

_____

_____

_____

Do you think Esther ever wanted to give up? Why or why not? _____

_____

_____

_____

_____

_____

_____

_____

_____

_____

_____

_____

_____

What would you have done if you were in Esther's shoes? How would you respond in a life-or-death situation? _____

_____

_____

_____

_____

_____

_____

_____

_____

_____

_____

_____

_____

_____

If someone talked to you about quitting something he/she started, would you encourage him/her to finish? Why or why not? _____

_____

_____

_____

_____

_____

_____

_____

_____

_____

_____

_____

Do you think that God test you? If so, how? If not, why? _____

_____

_____

_____

_____

_____

_____

_____

_____

_____

_____

_____

_____

_____

Fasting and Praying

Read each scripture and explain in your own words what each one means to you.

Matthew 17:20-21 _____

_____

_____

_____

_____

_____

_____

_____

_____

_____

Ezra 8:23 _____

_____

_____

_____

_____

_____

_____

_____

_____

When Esther called the people to fast and pray; what was the important of the fasting and praying? _____

_____

_____

_____

_____

_____

_____

_____

_____

_____

_____

_____

_____

_____

What is fasting and praying? How important are they? _____

_____

_____

_____

_____

_____

_____

_____

_____

_____

_____

_____

_____

What can you learn from Esther's example? _____

_____

_____

_____

_____

_____

_____

_____

_____

_____

_____

_____

Do you know how to pray? When should you pray? Why or why not? _____

_____

_____

_____

_____

_____

_____

_____

_____

_____

_____

_____

_____

_____

Summarize week one in a sentence. Do you feel it will help you in your daily life? Why or why not? _____

_____

_____

_____

_____

_____

_____

_____

_____

_____

_____

_____

_____

_____

_____

_____

_____

_____

WEEK 2

"But you are a chosen people, a royal priesthood, a holy nation, God's people, so that you may proclaim the mighty acts of him who called you out of darkness into his marvelous light."

—I Peter 2:2-10

Introduction of Esther's Values

You are valuable. Do you know this? Do you really know how valuable you are? Well, first of all, your value begins with the fact that you are made by the hand of the Creator, who created you in His very image. End of story! The discussion of the value of yourself is no longer. Right? Wrong.

Let me tell you; people are going to treat you as if you are not worth anything. They are going to make you question your value each day and try to diminish any value you may think you have. But, know this, everything about you is valuable. Your every thought, and your opinions, whether bad or good, will add value to your life. Either the bad thoughts and ideas will teach you not to do "that" again, or the kind thoughts and opinions will add value to your life.

Do not let people withdraw from your value. Every time someone tries to make a withdrawal, you make a more substantial deposit of cost to your life. Know your self-worth. It is yours, and no one has the right to take that away from you.

"Greatness is not measured by what a man or woman accomplishes, but by the opposition, he or she has overcome to reach his goals."
– Dorothy Height

Esther's Values

Day 1
- **Faith**
  - Mark 11:24
  - Hebrews 11:1

Day 2
- **Wisdom**
  - Proverbs 3:7
  - Ecclesiastes 2:26

Day 3
- **Strength**
  - Luke 1:45
  - Esther 4:14

Day 4
- **Submitting to God**
  - I Peter 5:5
  - Romans 12:2

Day 5
- **Humble/Humility**
  - 2 Chronicles 7:14
  - Mark 10:45

Be your
own hero.

Read each scripture and in your own words explain what each one means to you.

Mark 11:24 _____

_____
_____
_____
_____
_____
_____
_____
_____
_____

Hebrews 11:1 _____

_____
_____
_____
_____
_____
_____
_____
_____
_____
_____

Is believing the same as having faith? _____

_____

_____

_____

_____

_____

_____

_____

_____

_____

_____

Is faith important? Why or why not? _____

_____

_____

_____

_____

_____

_____

_____

_____

_____

_____

_____

_____

Is having faith in God difficult? Why or why not? _____

_____

_____

_____

_____

_____

_____

_____

_____

_____

_____

_____

_____

_____

_____

_____

_____

Read each scripture and in your own words explain what each one means to you.

Proverbs 3:7 _____

_____

_____

_____

_____

_____

_____

_____

_____

_____

Ecclesiastes 2:26 _____

_____

_____

_____

_____

_____

_____

_____

_____

_____

_____

What does it mean to have wisdom? _____

_____

_____

_____

_____

_____

_____

_____

_____

_____

_____

_____

_____

_____

Is there a difference between wisdom and knowledge? _____

_____

_____

_____

_____

_____

_____

_____

_____

_____

_____

_____

_____

Give an example of a situation when you did not make a wise decision. _____

_____

_____

_____

_____

_____

_____

_____

_____

_____

_____

_____

_____

_____

_____

_____

Strength

Read each scripture and in your own words explain what each one means to you.

Luke 1:45 _____
_____
_____
_____
_____
_____
_____
_____
_____
_____
_____

Esther 4:14 _____
_____
_____
_____
_____
_____
_____
_____
_____
_____
_____
_____

What is inner strength? _____

_____
_____
_____
_____
_____
_____
_____
_____
_____
_____
_____
_____

List some of your strengths and your weaknesses?

Strengths	**Weaknesses**
(1) _____	_____
(2) _____	_____
(3) _____	_____
(4) _____	_____
(5) _____	_____
(6) _____	_____

How can you work on each of your weaknesses? _____

_____

_____

_____

_____

_____

_____

_____

_____

_____

_____

_____

_____

_____

_____

_____

_____

_____

_____

_____

Submitting to God

Read each scripture and in your own words explain what each one means to you.

I Peter 5:5 _____

_____

_____

_____

_____

_____

_____

_____

_____

_____

Romans 12:2 _____

_____

_____

_____

_____

_____

_____

_____

_____

_____

_____

_____

How do you submit to God? _____

_____

_____

_____

_____

_____

_____

_____

_____

_____

_____

_____

_____

_____

_____

Should you only submit to God when good things happen in your life? _____

_____

_____

_____

_____

_____

_____

_____

_____

_____

_____

_____

_____

_____

What hinders you from walking in God's plan for your life? _____

_____

_____

_____

_____

_____

_____

_____

_____

_____

_____

_____

_____

_____

Read each scripture and in your own words explain what each one means to you.

2 Chronicles 7:14 _____

_____

_____

_____

_____

_____

_____

_____

_____

_____

Mark 10:45 _____

_____

_____

_____

_____

_____

_____

_____

_____

_____

_____

What does humility mean? Give examples. _____

_____

_____

_____

_____

_____

_____

_____

_____

_____

_____

_____

_____

_____

Is having pride more important than having humility? Why or why not? _____

_____

_____

_____

_____

_____

_____

_____

_____

_____

_____

_____

_____

How hard or easy is it to be humble? Why? _____
_____
_____
_____
_____
_____
_____
_____
_____
_____
_____
_____
_____
_____
_____

Summarize week two in a sentence. Do you feel it will help you in your daily
life? Why or why not? _____
_____
_____
_____
_____
_____
_____
_____
_____
_____
_____
_____
_____
_____
_____

WEEK 3

"She opens her mouth in wisdom, and the teaching of kindness is on her tongue."

—Proverbs 31:26

Introduction of Esther's Characteristics

Dictionary definition of character is the stable and distinctive qualities built into an individual's life that determines a response regardless of circumstances. In the Martin Luther King Jr. "I Have a Dream" speech he states, "I have a dream that my four little children will one day live in a nation where they will not be judged by the color of their skin but the content of their character." Have you ever stopped to think about the content of your character? What does that look like?

Your character is built on how you deal with others and with situations. It is based on the choices and decisions you make. It all starts with what you think within yourselves. Your character is more than your reputation. Your character is what you do when no one else is around. Your reputation is what others see you as.

You are not born with character, and it is not a hereditary trait. A character can't be defined by doing an act for one time only. Your moral decision and moral judgment determine character. Your character is built from within, and it is the conscious choices you make every day that will strengthen your character that is pleasing to yourself and God. Try to do what's right, and have positive inner thoughts, and these will develop your character.

"Mistakes are a fact of life. It is the response to the error that counts."
- Nikki Giovanni

Esther's Characteristics

Day 1
- ♡ **Grace**
  - ✂ I Peter 5:10
  - ✂ Ephesians 2:4-9

Day 2
- ♡ **Virtue**
  - ✂ Philippians 4:8
  - ✂ Psalm 41:12

Day 3
- ♡ **Forgiveness**
  - ✂ Colossians 3:13
  - ✂ Matthew 6:14-15

Day 4
- ♡ **Sincere**
  - ✂ Joshua 24:14
  - ✂ Romans 12:9

Day 5
- ♡ **Patience**
  - ✂ Psalm 4:4
  - ✂ James 5:7-8

Shine bright as a diamond.

Grace

Read each scripture and in your own words explain what each one means to you.

I Peter 5:10 _____

_____

_____

_____

_____

_____

_____

_____

_____

_____

Ephesians 2:4-9 _____

_____

_____

_____

_____

_____

_____

_____

_____

_____

_____

_____

_____

What is grace and when is it provided by God? _____

_____

_____

_____

_____

_____

_____

_____

_____

_____

_____

_____

_____

Should you only submit to God when good things happen in your life? _____

_____

_____

_____

_____

_____

_____

_____

_____

_____

_____

_____

_____

_____

_____

Describe what "GRACE" means to you as an acronym.

G_____

R_____

A_____

C_____

E_____

Virtue

Read each scripture and in your own words explain what each one means to you.

Philippians 4:8 _____

_____

_____

_____

_____

_____

_____

_____

_____

_____

Psalms 41:12 _____

_____

_____

_____

_____

_____

_____

_____

_____

_____

_____

_____

What does being self-assured/confident mean to you? _____

_____

_____

_____

_____

_____

_____

_____

_____

_____

_____

_____

_____

_____

Has someone ever caused you to lose confidence in yourself in a situation?
How did you handle that situation? _____

_____

_____

_____

_____

_____

_____

_____

_____

_____

_____

_____

_____

_____

Do you ever compare yourself with others? Why or why not? _____

_____

_____

_____

_____

_____

_____

_____

_____

_____

_____

_____

_____

_____

_____

Forgiveness

Read each scripture and in your own words explain what each one means to you.

Colossians 3:15 _____

_____

_____

_____

_____

_____

_____

_____

_____

_____

Matthew 6:14-15 _____

_____

_____

_____

_____

_____

_____

_____

_____

_____

_____

_____

What is forgiveness? _____

_____

_____

_____

_____

_____

_____

_____

_____

_____

_____

_____

The Bible states that you should love your enemies and pray for those who persecute you. How easy or difficult is this to do this? Why or why not? _____

_____

_____

_____

_____

_____

_____

_____

_____

_____

_____

_____

_____

What should you do if you do not know how to forgive? _____

_____

_____

_____

_____

_____

_____

_____

_____

_____

_____

_____

_____

_____

_____

_____

Sincere

Read each scripture and in your own words explain what each one means to you.

Joshua 24:14 _____

_____

_____

_____

_____

_____

_____

_____

_____

_____

Romans 12:9 _____

_____

_____

_____

_____

_____

_____

_____

_____

_____

_____

What does being sincere mean to you? _____

_____

_____

_____

_____

_____

_____

_____

_____

_____

_____

_____

_____

_____

_____

_____

Describe a time when you were not sincere in words and/or actions. What was
the outcome of that situation? _____

_____

_____

_____

_____

_____

_____

_____

_____

_____

_____

_____

_____

_____

How do you plan to be sincerer in your daily life? _____

_____

_____

_____

_____

_____

_____

_____

_____

_____

_____

_____

_____

_____

_____

_____

Read each scripture and in your own words explain what each one means to you.

Psalm 4:4 _____

_____

_____

_____

_____

_____

_____

_____

_____

_____

_____

James 5:7-8 _____

_____

_____

_____

_____

_____

_____

_____

_____

_____

_____

_____

What situations make you lose patience? _____

_____

_____

_____

_____

_____

_____

_____

_____

_____

_____

_____

_____

What are you most patient about? _____

_____

_____

_____

_____

_____

_____

_____

_____

_____

_____

_____

_____

_____

_____

When you have been praying for a long time to God for something to happen in your life, and received no answer, do you feel God is not listening? Why or why not? _____

_____

_____

_____

_____

_____

_____

_____

_____

_____

_____

_____

Summarize week three in a sentence. Do you feel it will help you in your daily life? Why or why not? _____

_____

_____

_____

_____

_____

_____

_____

_____

_____

_____

_____

_____

WEEK 4

"For the Lord gives wisdom; from His mouth come knowledge and understanding."

—Proverbs 2:6

Introduction of Esther's Principles

Having principle is the root of all you do and what you believe. It is the foundation on which you stand. It is something that is permanent, entirely sufficient, unconditional, and full of hope. It is the very foundation for which the Word of God is built upon. Jeremiah 17: 8 says, "For he shall be as a tree planted by the waters, which spreads out its roots by the river and shall not fear when heat comes, but its leaf shall be green; and shall not be careful in the year of drought, neither shall cease from yielding fruit." Having principle is like a tree that is planted by water.

Being principled is having rules and regulations in your life, to keep you inline, to ensure you are doing what is right, what is Godly. Why should you be a person of principle? Having principle means that you try to make the right decision, Godly decision when faced with a tough situation, or when life seems to be spinning out of control. It is the very thing that keeps you grounded: honesty, equality, integrity, and trusting God.

"Deal with yourself as an individual worthy of respect, and make everyone else deal with you the same."
– Nikki Giovanni

Esther's Principles

Day 1
- ♡ **Serving others**
  - ☙ Philippians 2:5-7
  - ☙ Mark 9:35

Day 2
- ♡ **What gets written gets done (you need a written plan)**
  - ☙ Jeremiah 30:2
  - ☙ Joshua 24:26

Day 3
- ♡ **Understanding your situation/When to speak/Choosing your words wisely**
  - ☙ Proverbs 13:3
  - ☙ I Corinthians 2:9-12

Day 4
- ♡ **Gifts/Talents**
  - ☙ Romans 12:6
  - ☙ Ephesians 2:10

Day 5
- ♡ **Trusting God**
  - ☙ Psalm 56:4
  - ☙ Isaiah 40:28-31

Believe in
yourself.

Serving Others

Read each scripture and in your own words explain what each one means to you.

Philippians 2:5-7 _____

_____

_____

_____

_____

_____

_____

_____

_____

_____

Mark 9:35 _____

_____

_____

_____

_____

_____

_____

_____

_____

_____

_____

_____

What does serving others mean? _____

_____

_____

_____

_____

_____

_____

_____

_____

_____

_____

_____

Is helping others easy all the time? Why or why not? _____

_____

_____

_____

_____

_____

_____

_____

_____

_____

_____

_____

_____

Have you served/helped anyone in the past week? Who? What did you do? ___

_____

_____

_____

_____

_____

_____

_____

_____

_____

_____

_____

_____

_____

_____

What Gets Written Gets Done

Read each scripture and in your own words explain what each one means to you.

Jeremiah 30:2 _____

_____

_____

_____

_____

_____

_____

_____

_____

_____

Joshua 24:26_____

_____

_____

_____

_____

_____

_____

_____

_____

_____

_____

_____

What does "what gets written gets done" mean to you? _____

_____

_____

_____

_____

_____

_____

_____

_____

_____

_____

_____

_____

How important is it to have a written plan for your life purpose? _____

_____

_____

_____

_____

_____

_____

_____

_____

_____

_____

_____

_____

_____

_____

What was God's written plan for Esther's life? _____
_____
_____
_____
_____
_____
_____
_____
_____
_____
_____
_____
_____
_____
_____

Choose Your Words Wisely

Read each scripture and in your own words explain what each one means to you.

Proverbs 13:3 _____

_____

_____

_____

_____

_____

_____

_____

_____

I Corinthians 2:9-12 _____

_____

_____

_____

_____

_____

_____

_____

_____

_____

_____

_____

Have you ever examined a situation closely before responding? Why or why not?

_____

_____

_____

_____

_____

_____

_____

_____

_____

_____

_____

_____

Name a situation where you've hurt someone's feelings through your words? Did you apologize afterwards? Why or why not? _____

_____

_____

_____

_____

_____

_____

_____

_____

_____

_____

_____

_____

_____

Write an apology to someone who you have not apologized to. _____

_____

_____

_____

_____

_____

_____

_____

_____

_____

_____

_____

_____

_____

_____

_____

_____

Gifts/Talents

Read each scripture and in your own words explain what each one means to you.

Romans 12:6 _____

_____

_____

_____

_____

_____

_____

_____

_____

_____

Ephesians 2:10 _____

_____

_____

_____

_____

_____

_____

_____

_____

What is the biblical definition for the words below? What is Webster's definition?

Talent (Biblical Definition): _____

_____

_____

_____

_____

_____

Spiritual Gift (Biblical Definition): _____

_____

_____

_____

_____

_____

Talent (Webster's Definition): _____

_____

_____

_____

_____

_____

Spiritual Gift (Webster's Definition): _____

_____

_____

_____

_____

_____

What is the difference between "talent" and "spiritual gift"? _____

_____

_____

_____

_____

_____

_____

_____

_____

_____

List some of your talent(s) and spiritual gift(s).

Talent(s)	**Spiritual Gift(s)**
_____	_____
_____	_____
_____	_____
_____	_____

Read each scripture and in your own words explain what each one means to you.

Psalm 56:4 _____

_____

_____

_____

_____

_____

_____

_____

_____

Isaiah 40:28-31 _____

_____

_____

_____

_____

_____

_____

_____

_____

_____

_____

Why is trusting God so important? _____

_____

_____

_____

_____

_____

_____

_____

_____

_____

_____

How do you know if God is with you when you go through a difficult time?

_____

_____

_____

_____

_____

_____

_____

_____

_____

_____

_____

_____

Do you have a hard time trusting others? Why or why not? _____

_____

_____

_____

_____

_____

_____

_____

_____

_____

_____

_____

_____

The Book of Esther does not mention God. Why do you think this is so? How do you know He was present in her life and the Book of Esther? _____

_____

_____

_____

_____

_____

_____

_____

_____

_____

_____

_____

_____

_____

Summarize week four in a sentence. Do you feel it will help you in your daily life? Why or why not? _____

_____

_____

_____

_____

_____

_____

_____

_____

_____

_____

_____

_____

_____

_____

WEEK 5

"But you will receive power when the Holy Spirit has come upon you, and you will be my witnesses in Jerusalem and all Judea and Samaria, and to the end of the earth."

—Acts 1:8

Introduction of Esther's Mission

When you hear the word mission, what do you think about? Do you think about a mission trip? Do you think about *Mission Impossible*? Do you think about being on a mission? Mission is an important assignment carried out for a purpose; it's purpose can be political, religious, commercial, or personal.

Everyone has some type of mission in their life. Do you know what your mission is in your life? Some people will realize theirs sooner in life than others. But, whatever that mission is, God will supply you with what you need to carry it out. You just need to be available, because God will give you the ability to carry out his plan for your life.

"I choose to make the rest of my life the best of my life."

- Louise Hay

Esther's Mission

Day 1

- ♡ **Empower**
  - ⚘ Proverbs 31:25
  - ⚘ Psalm 46:5

Day 2

- ♡ **Encourage**
  - ⚘ Isaiah 41:10
  - ⚘ Psalm 55:22

Day 3

- ♡ **Evangelize**
  - ⚘ Mark 16:15
  - ⚘ Matthew 28:19-20

Day 4

- ♡ **Elevate**
  - ⚘ Luke 14:11
  - ⚘ I Peter 5:6

Day 5

- ♡ **Equip**
  - ⚘ Luke 4: 18-19
  - ⚘ Hebrews 13:20-21

I can and I will. Watch me.

Empower

Read each scripture and in your own words explain what each one means to you.

Proverbs 1:25 _____

_____

_____

_____

_____

_____

_____

_____

_____

_____

Psalm 46:5 _____

_____

_____

_____

_____

_____

_____

_____

_____

_____

_____

What does be empowered mean to you? _____

_____

_____

_____

_____

_____

_____

_____

_____

_____

_____

_____

_____

_____

Has anyone empowered you? Who? How? _____

_____

_____

_____

_____

_____

_____

_____

_____

_____

_____

_____

_____

_____

What causes you to be the best version of yourself? _____

_____

_____

_____

_____

_____

_____

_____

_____

_____

_____

_____

_____

_____

_____

_____

_____

_____

_____

_____

_____

_____

_____

_____

_____

_____

_____

_____

_____

_____

_____

_____

_____

Encourage

Read each scripture and in your own words explain what each one means to you.

Isaiah 4:10 _____

_____

_____

_____

_____

_____

_____

_____

_____

_____

_____

Psalm 55:22 _____

_____

_____

_____

_____

_____

_____

_____

_____

_____

_____

_____

How do you think God encourages you? _____

_____

_____

_____

_____

_____

_____

_____

_____

_____

_____

_____

_____

How do you feel or respond when someone tries to encourage you? _____

_____

_____

_____

_____

_____

_____

_____

_____

_____

_____

_____

_____

_____

_____

How would you encourage a friend who has just lost his/her parent? _____

_____

_____

_____

_____

_____

_____

_____

_____

_____

_____

_____

_____

_____

Evangelize

Read each scripture and in your own words explain what each one means to you.

Mark 16:15 _____

_____
_____
_____
_____
_____
_____
_____
_____
_____

Matthew 28:19-20 _____

_____
_____
_____
_____
_____
_____
_____
_____
_____
_____

What is the definition of evangelize? _____

_____

_____

_____

_____

_____

_____

_____

_____

_____

_____

_____

Do you teach your friends about the Word of God? Why or why not? _____

_____

_____

_____

_____

_____

_____

_____

_____

_____

_____

_____

_____

Do you think much about your spiritual life and spiritual growth? Why or why not?

_____

_____

_____

_____

_____

_____

_____

_____

_____

_____

_____

_____

_____

_____

_____

_____

_____

_____

_____

_____

_____

_____

_____

_____

Read each scripture and in your own words explain what each one means to you.

Luke 14:11 _____

_____

_____

_____

_____

_____

_____

_____

_____

_____

I Peter 5:6 _____

_____

_____

_____

_____

_____

_____

_____

_____

_____

_____

_____

What are the ways to be spiritually elevated? _____

_____
_____
_____
_____
_____
_____
_____
_____
_____
_____
_____
_____
_____

What is the importance of spiritual growth? _____

_____
_____
_____
_____
_____
_____
_____
_____
_____
_____
_____
_____
_____
_____

Is there a distinction between spirituality and religion? _____

_____

_____

_____

_____

_____

_____

_____

_____

_____

_____

_____

_____

What preparation does God take us through? _____

_____

_____

_____

_____

_____

_____

_____

_____

_____

_____

_____

_____

_____

Equip

Read each scripture and in your own words explain what each one means to you.

Luke 4:18-19 _____

_____

_____

_____

_____

_____

_____

_____

_____

Hebrews 13:20-21 _____

_____

_____

_____

_____

_____

_____

_____

_____

_____

_____

Are you equipped to handle adversity? In what ways are you equipped? _____

_____

_____

_____

_____

_____

_____

_____

_____

_____

_____

It is said that when God calls you to do a work, He gives you what you need. How do you think God does each one below? Provide a scripture to support your answer.

Equips: _____

_____

_____

_____

_____

_____

Enables: _____

_____

_____

_____

_____

_____

Provides: _____

_____

_____

_____

_____

_____

_____

Qualifies: _____

_____

_____

_____

_____

_____

_____

Summarize week five in a sentence. Do you feel it will help you in your daily life? Why or why not? _____

_____

_____

_____

_____

_____

_____

_____

_____

_____

_____

_____

_____

WEEK 6

"I praise you, for I am fearfully and wonderfully made. Wonderful are your works; my soul knows it very well."

– Psalms 139:14

Introduction of What Are You Made Of

What are you made of? You are made up of your values, characteristics, principles, potential, and purpose. These are the things that make you fearfully and wonderfully made. Have you stopped to think what this means? Being "fearfully and wonderfully made"? "Fearfully" is to have respect for God, thanking God for the body and life for which he gave you. Too often you may not like what you see in the mirror, but, remember who created you.

"Wonderfully" means that you are uniquely designed. God made you special, and He has a purpose and a plan for you. God formed you and created you as his masterpiece for a purpose. God has put together this particular recipe to create for you. It is a recipe that is not handed down and cannot be given to anyone else.

As you go about your life, do not let anyone speak negatively into your life and plant a seed of doubt about who you are. You are fearfully and wonderfully made for such a time as this. What are you made of? Sugar and spice and everything nice.

"We are all gifted. That is our inheritance."
— Ethel Waters

What Are You Made Of?

Day 1

- ♡ **Values**
  - ⚹ Mathew 26:14-15
  - ⚹ II Corinthians 5:17

Day 2

- ♡ **Characteristics**
  - ⚹ Matthew 6:33-34
  - ⚹ Proverbs 31:30

Day 3

- ♡ **Principles**
  - ⚹ Matthew 6:5
  - ⚹ Galatians 4:9

Day 4

- ♡ **Potential**
  - ⚹ John 10:10
  - ⚹ I Peter 2:9-10

Day 5

- ♡ **Purpose**
  - ⚹ Exodus 9:16
  - ⚹ Proverbs 20:5

Aspire to

inspire.

Value

Read each scripture and in your own words explain what each one means to you.

Matthew 26:14-15 _____

_____

_____

_____

_____

_____

_____

_____

_____

II Corinthians 5:17 _____

_____

_____

_____

_____

_____

_____

_____

_____

_____

What are your values? _____

_____

_____

_____

_____

_____

_____

_____

_____

_____

_____

_____

_____

What values have your parents taught you? _____

_____

_____

_____

_____

_____

_____

_____

_____

_____

_____

_____

_____

_____

What are ethical values? Why are they important? _____

_____

_____

_____

_____

_____

_____

_____

_____

_____

_____

_____

_____

Do you know the values you hold? _____

_____

_____

_____

_____

_____

_____

_____

_____

_____

_____

_____

_____

_____

Characteristics

Read each scripture and in your own words explain what each one means to you.

Matthew 6:33-34 _____

_____

_____

_____

_____

_____

_____

_____

_____

_____

_____

Proverbs 31:30 _____

_____

_____

_____

_____

_____

_____

_____

_____

_____

_____

_____

List some of your characteristics that are unique to you. _____

_____

_____

_____

_____

_____

_____

_____

_____

_____

_____

_____

_____

What is your definition of character? Is it important? _____

_____

_____

_____

_____

_____

_____

_____

_____

_____

_____

_____

_____

_____

_____

Can your character be malicious (hateful)? _____

_____

_____

_____

_____

_____

_____

_____

_____

_____

_____

_____

_____

_____

If you found $500, what would you do with it? Why? Does this define your character? _____

_____

_____

_____

_____

_____

_____

_____

_____

_____

_____

_____

_____

Principles

Read each scripture and in your own words explain what each one means to you.

Matthew 6:5 _____

_____

_____

_____

_____

_____

_____

_____

_____

_____

Galatians 4:9 _____

_____

_____

_____

_____

_____

_____

_____

_____

_____

_____

_____

What does having principles mean? _____

_____

_____

_____

_____

_____

_____

_____

_____

_____

_____

_____

What are Christian morals? _____

_____

_____

_____

_____

_____

_____

_____

_____

_____

_____

_____

Give examples of principles or conducts that are moral and some that are immoral.

Moral   **Immoral**

_____   _____

_____   _____

_____   _____

_____   _____

Read each scripture and in your own words explain what each one means to you.

John 10:10 _____

_____

_____

_____

_____

_____

_____

_____

_____

_____

I Peter 2:9-10 _____

_____

_____

_____

_____

_____

_____

_____

_____

_____

_____

What is the definition of potential? _____

_____

_____

_____

_____

_____

_____

_____

_____

What potential(s) do you see in front of you? _____

_____

_____

_____

_____

_____

_____

_____

_____

What possibilities do you have inside of you? _____

_____

_____

_____

_____

_____

_____

_____

_____

Purpose

Read each scripture and in your own words explain what each one means to you.

Exodus 9:16 _____

_____

_____

_____

_____

_____

_____

_____

_____

_____

Proverbs 20:5 _____

_____

_____

_____

_____

_____

_____

_____

_____

_____

_____

_____

What is my purpose for my life? Why is it important? _____

_____

_____

_____

_____

_____

_____

_____

_____

_____

_____

_____

_____

_____

_____

What is God's purpose for my life? _____

_____

_____

_____

_____

_____

_____

_____

_____

_____

_____

_____

_____

_____

_____

_____

What am I afraid of when it comes to pursing my purpose? _____

_____

_____

_____

_____

_____

_____

_____

_____

_____

_____

_____

_____

Summarize week one in a sentence. Do you feel it will help you in your daily life? Why or why not? _____

_____

_____

_____

_____

_____

_____

_____

_____

_____

_____

_____

_____

WEEK 7

"If I didn't define myself for myself,
I would be crunched into other people's
fantasies for me and eaten alive."
– Audre Lorde

Introduction to Defining Yourself

Adjustments are necessary to get you on track, and for you to live your life with meaning. You may need to adjust your attitude, values, characteristics, motives, and/or principles. Adjustments are necessary; make them and continue to push forward.

Adjustments are meant to help you grow and progress through your life. Some adjustments are painful. Life will give you some blows. Some blows will knock you down; get back up and keep fighting. The key words here are "get back up." A rule in boxing is that if you get knocked down in the ring, there is a ten-count period during which you must get back up on your feet. Give yourself that ten-count... 1, 2, 3, 4, 5, 6, 7, 8, 9, 10. Get up. Get back on your feet and start fighting. Fight all those things that keep you from your purpose, all that slows you down—negative people, negative conversations, self-doubt, hatred, anger. Whatever it is, keep moving your feet and keep swinging. Fight for your joy and peace, fight for your family, fight for yourself, fight for your purpose.

The adjustments will bring you closer to living a life of purpose. Webster's definition states that "purpose" is the reason for which something is created or for which something exists. The reason you exit is your purpose. So what is your goal, you ask? Living with intention means living a life that you know you are expected to live. It manifests through every thought and action. What is it that keeps you going? It's your heart's desire that does not allow you to quit. Even when there are hardships, trials, and tribulations, you must keep going, because you are just that much closer to your purpose.

"A woman's gifts will make room for her."
— Hattie McDaniel

Defining Yourself

Day 1
- ♡ **Me**

Day 2
- ♡ **Passion**

Day 3
- ♡ **Vision**

Day 4
- ♡ **Adjustment**

Day 5
- ♡ **Letter to Self**

Be thankful.

Who am I? _____

_____

_____

_____

_____

_____

_____

_____

_____

_____

_____

_____

_____

_____

_____

_____

_____

_____

_____

_____

_____

_____

_____

_____

_____

_____

_____

_____

Why did God create me in his image? _____

_____

_____

_____

_____

_____

_____

_____

_____

_____

_____

_____

_____

_____

What is my mission in my life? Why? _____

_____

_____

_____

_____

_____

_____

_____

_____

_____

_____

_____

_____

_____

For each letter in **"MISSION"** write a word describing yourself to support your mission statement.

M_____

I_____

S_____

S_____

I_____

O_____

N_____

Passion

What is the definition of passion? _____

_____

_____

_____

_____

_____

_____

_____

_____

_____

Is having passion important? Why or why not? _____

_____

_____

_____

_____

_____

_____

_____

_____

_____

_____

_____

_____

What am I passionate about? Why? _____

_____

_____

_____

_____

_____

_____

_____

_____

_____

_____

_____

_____

_____

What difference would I like to make in this world? Why? _____

_____

_____

_____

_____

_____

_____

_____

_____

_____

_____

_____

_____

_____

_____

What does the title of the book mean to you? _____

_____

_____

_____

_____

_____

_____

_____

_____

_____

_____

_____

Has this journal helped me in any way? Why or why not? _____

_____

_____

_____

_____

_____

_____

_____

_____

_____

_____

_____

_____

_____

Vision

I had an English teacher in high school (Mrs. James) who would say, "Excuses only satisfies those who make them." What excused do you make? Do you make an excuse to justify or defend bad behavior, a decision, or action? _____

_____

_____

_____

_____

_____

_____

_____

_____

_____

_____

_____

_____

_____

_____

_____

_____

_____

_____

_____

_____

Create a bucket list. (A bucket list comprises experiences or achievements that you hope to accomplish in the future.)

(1) _____

(2) _____

(3) _____

(4) _____

(5) _____

Try and stop me!

Write an action plan for each of your items on the bucket list of how you plan to achieve each one.

(1) _____

(2) _____

(3) _____

(4) _____

(5) _____

Write an affirmation. Put each of your affirmations on an index card or post-it, and put it in a place that reminds you that you are a queen.

I am _____

I am _____

I am _____

I am _____

I am _____

I am _____

I am _____

AFFIRMATION

I can do all things through Christ who strengthens me. I will reach the unreachable, touch the untouchable, and see the invisible because . . .

I am Anointed!   I am Confident!

I am Courageous!

I am an Overcomer!   I am Beautiful!

I am Empowered!

I am Extraordinary!   I am Empowered!

I Simply Am!

Adjustments

What sacrifices or adjustments am I willing to make for my purpose?

Sacrifice _____

_____

_____

Why? _____

_____

_____

_____

_____

_____

_____

Sacrifice _____

_____

_____

Why? _____

_____

_____

_____

_____

_____

How easy or difficult is it to accept change and adjust to life? _____

_____
_____
_____
_____
_____
_____
_____
_____
_____
_____
_____
_____

How easy or difficult it is to change my attitude about something or someone on a daily base? _____

_____
_____
_____
_____
_____
_____
_____
_____
_____
_____
_____
_____

How do I react when someone says, "You have a negative attitude"? _____

_____

_____

_____

_____

_____

_____

_____

_____

_____

_____

_____

_____

What am I thankful for? _____

_____

_____

_____

_____

_____

_____

_____

_____

_____

_____

_____

_____

_____

Write a letter to yourself five years from now.

Date of Letter: _____

Dear Self,

_____

_____

_____

_____

_____

_____

_____

_____

_____

_____

_____

_____

_____

_____

_____

_____

_____

_____

_____

_____

_____

_____

"Every great dream begins with a dreamer. Always remember, you have within you the strength, the patience, and the passion to reach for the stars to change the world."
– Harriet Tubman

Reflection II

Dear Mirror on the wall, I am a **"QUEEN"** after all!

Every day, I stared into the mirror, always asking myself the same questions Who am I? Is this life worth living? Am I a positive influence on someone else? Will I be brave through tough situations? Am I good enough? Am I living without a purpose? What is my goal?

I spoke to the mirror as though it could comprehend my questions. Why are you silent? Why do you merely stare at me? How long am I to wait before you answer my questions? Its silence troubled me. Then, I heard a small, soft voice say, "Only you can answer these questions. It's your life, and you must find your purpose. Only you can discover your true purpose in life—the reason you are here in the first place. Only you can answer why you exist. Why do you wait for others to validate your existence? Are you defined by what they think of you?"

Today, I stare at the mirror, not to ask questions but to provide the answers only I can give. They were inside me all along. I will no longer let people, places, or things intimidate me, victimize me, or spread negativity in my life. I am better than good enough! I am a royal priestess! On this day, I rise, and I shine because I am a queen after all.

I dare you to be GREAT.

Dear Readers,

Is this the moment for which you are created? I pray this book, *Let Me Adjust My Crown and Go Get My Purpose* has blessed your life, even if only a little.

My prayer is that Esther's life will resonate in your mind, body, heart, and soul. I want Esther's life to make you realize how fearfully and wonderfully created you have been. No one on this earth can be you better than you. God has designed you in precisely the way you are supposed to be. Embrace and love yourself!

I want you to know that there will be times in your life when certain circumstances will hurt, harm, and put you in danger. In such moments, you may feel like you've lost your best friend or that your entire world has come crashing down. Such moments can alter your life—for better or for worse.

Let each new situation in your life help you grow stronger and wiser. Don't let the circumstances of your life stop you from attaining your purpose. They may stall you for a while or slow you down, but don't stop. Regardless of the circumstance, learn the lesson you are supposed to learn. Let it empower, encourage, educate, elevate, and equip you to move forward in your journey towards higher heights and deeper depths of God's plan for your life. Perhaps this is the moment for which you came into being—the moment you arrive at your royal position. So adjust your crown, for this is your moment!

Thank you,
Sheila Prioleau

Made in the USA
Columbia, SC
24 March 2019